YO-EFZ-367

NASDTEC OUTCOME-BASED STANDARDS AND PORTFOLIO ASSESSMENT©

"Promoting Systemic Change in Teacher Education and Certification"

OUTCOME-BASED TEACHER EDUCATION STANDARDS FOR THE ELEMENTARY AND MIDDLE LEVELS

ADOPTED BY THE
NATIONAL ASSOCIATION OF STATE DIRECTORS OF
TEACHER EDUCATION AND CERTIFICATION (NASDTEC)

JUNE 1992

➤ Developed by the NASDTEC Joint Standards and Middle Level Committee ➤

KENDALL/HUNT PUBLISHING COMPANY
2460 Kerper Boulevard   P.O. Box 539   Dubuque, Iowa 52004-0539

TABLE OF CONTENTS

SECTION - 1

SYSTEMIC CHANGE IN TEACHER EDUCATION AND CERTIFICATION

Introduction

Since 1928 the National Association of State Directors of Teacher Education and Certification (NASDTEC) has been committed to the development of qualified educational personnel. NASDTEC has provided leadership in the development, implementation, and evaluation of standards for teacher education. Its membership constitutes the 50 states, the District of Columbia, Puerto Rico, the territories, and the Department of Defense Schools.

Throughout its history NASDTEC has maintained professional standards that are current, based on effective practices, and representative of the diversity of teacher preparation programs across the nation. NASDTEC has also been actively supporting the Interstate Certification Contract Administrators' Association whereby 31 states and the District of Columbia work together to facilitate the movement of practicing teachers across state lines.

The past few years have seen renewed interest in education by the federal government and at the state level. This concern has culminated in major reform initiatives, such as *America 2000*, which has established six National Education Goals that have been adopted by a majority of the states.

These reform efforts focus on the outcomes of public education and are engaging not only the federal and state governments but also the business community and educators at all levels in designing new programs to assist students in meeting these outcomes.

NASDTEC supports the belief that the role of government agencies and professional associations must be to provide leadership related to the outcomes of public education but it also recognizes that the state has the fundamental responsibility for the certification/ licensure of teachers. The development of the NASDTEC outcome-based standards is a direct response to the emerging reform efforts throughout the United States.

For over twenty years NASDTEC has developed standards that have identified areas of study and requirements that colleges and universities must meet in order to have approved programs. These standards have largely shaped the programs for the preparation of teachers across the United States. In this document, NASDTEC takes a major step by shifting program approval to outcome-based standards.

As you read this document, it will become evident that a movement to outcome-based standards calls into question long standing procedures and beliefs. Changes must occur if outcome-based standards are to be implemented.

The standards also challenge the fundamental nature of a state's "approved program" approach to teacher education. While the outcome-based standards are designed to provide a framework for the approval of college and university teacher education programs, the standards also could be used by states to approve alternative programs of preparation or even to design licensure examinations that could be used in lieu of or in addition to traditional approved programs at colleges and universities.

Persons who have reviewed drafts of these standards have also proposed that they could be used by states or school districts in conjunction with induction programs. Such programs could add even greater relevance to the standards as the conditions and culture of the school could provide a truly "authentic" context for the portfolio assessments. In addition, data would be able to be collected from the "clients" listed in each standard to determine if the "purpose" of the standard had actually been met.

These standards have been developed through the combined efforts of the NASDTEC Standards and Middle Level Committees, chaired by Roger C. Mouritsen, Utah. The Committees include Betty Fry, Florida; Nancy Green, Kansas; Mary Hendrick Conley, Washington, D.C.; Mike McKibbin, California; John Nichelson, Ohio; Dianne Worthy, Kentucky; and Susan Tave Zelman, Massachusetts. The Committees received significant assistance from Nicholas Hobar and Robert Gabrys, WORKFORCE 2000, INC. who served as consultants to the committees and conceptualized the initial model for the standards.

In addition to thanking the above individuals, NASDTEC wishes also to publicly acknowledge and note its appreciation to the Carnegie Corporation of New York which provided a grant to NASDTEC to develop the Middle Level Standards.

Six of the nine state representatives that reviewed the first draft of these standards reported they were willing and anxious to field test the actual implementation of the standards during the 1992-93 school year. We are hopeful that their efforts will be joined by other NASDTEC states.

NASDTEC is now developing outcome-based standards for secondary programs and will be addressing special education standards next. We are anxious to receive reactions from individuals and organizations that choose to use these standards. The NASDTEC Standards Committee has as its mission the constant review, improvement, and development of standards. With this publication, NASDTEC adds its resources to the movement toward the development of outcome-based programs for school students now emerging across the United States.

While strongly supportive of these outcome-based standards, NASDTEC wishes to emphasize that no single approach to teacher education or set of standards will be able to guarantee that all of the intangibles needed to produce an excellent teacher will be in place. Selection criteria established for admission to a teacher education program or for certification or for employment decisions must be married to any set of standards. Teaching candidates can be educated to learn and demonstrate required knowledges and skills. However, a personal sense of responsibility, a commitment to children, and the stamina to persist in school systems overwhelmed by challenges are essential characteristics that must be addressed primarily through selection procedures.

NASDTEC also recognizes the rapidly emerging diversity in America's society. The millions of immigrants who came to the United States during the 1980s have been added to our country's already rich mixture of cultures and nationalities. The outcome-based standards are designed to prepare teachers who will be able to help all students--no matter what their backgrounds and nationalities--succeed in school and in life. Issues related to multiculturalism and cultural diversity, however, are not addressed as separate outcomes. The emphasis in the outcome-based standards is on role performances and job analyses of beginning teachers. The teacher must understand the curriculum and instruct students in ways that are sensitive to the country's culturally diverse population--these values are embedded in the "curriculum" and "instruction" standards.

These outcome-based standards represent the collective efforts of hundreds of educators throughout the United States. Developed initially by the NASDTEC Standards and Middle Level Committees, the drafts have been shared with and reviewed by educators in every state, elementary and middle level teachers, state teachers associations, representatives of governor's task forces and business roundtable committees, the INTASC Standards Drafting Committee of the Council of Chief State School Officers, the Unit Accreditation Board of the National Council for the Accreditation of Teacher Education, the boards of directors of the National Education Association and the American Association of Colleges for Teacher Education, and the National Board for Professional Teaching Standards. Many of the persons who have reviewed the drafts have been excited about the possibility for change and improvement. Some have raised questions (many of which have resulted in revisions in the document you now see), and some believe a shift to outcome-based standards will be too extreme a break with existing policies. The reform efforts in education now unleashed across many states are also extreme and present many challenges. This effort by NASDTEC complements the efforts of those states devoted to reforming an entire state's educational system.

On behalf of NASDTEC and the hard work of its members, it is with great personal pleasure that we are able to offer to member states and other educators "Outcome-based Teacher Education Standards for the Elementary and Middle Levels."

Theodore E. Andrews
President, NASDTEC

Outcome-Based Standards

The National Association of State Directors of Teacher Education and Certification (NASDTEC) is pleased to offer to its member states and to other interested educators these newly developed outcome-based standards for the approval of teacher education programs. The format for the standards is dramatically different from NASDTEC standards in the past. The focus is on what the beginning teacher should be able to do, think, and feel; not on what the prospective teacher should study. It is NASDTEC's strong belief that a solid set of outcome-based standards that can be used or adapted by individual states will eliminate or significantly reduce dictates to institutions of higher education related to resources, faculty, and curriculum.

Many states are now adopting outcome-based standards for public school students. The NASDTEC standards for the approval of programs for elementary and middle level teachers are compatible with these related efforts. In addition, NASDTEC's efforts are also linked to those of the National Council for the Accreditation of Teacher Education (NCATE) and the National Board for Professional Teaching Standards in their search for strong measures that impact licensure and that "... establish high and rigorous standards for what teachers should know and be able to do...to advance related education reforms for the purpose of improving student learning in American schools" (National Board for Professional Teaching Standards, 1991).

Underlying Assumptions of Outcome-Based Standards

According to Spady and Marshall (1991), outcomes must meet four driving assumptions. Those assumptions were modified for teacher education and applied in developing outcome-based teacher education standards for NASDTEC at the elementary and middle learning levels.

- Outcomes are demonstrations of learning, not the names of teaching specializations, college course content, concepts, programs, or themes;

- Learning demonstrations occur in settings, and settings add their own conditions and challenges to the demonstration;

- Outcomes are culminating demonstrations of significant components of the beginning teaching role on-the-job in a public school classroom;

- Exit outcomes are the ultimate culminating outcomes in a curricular design and professional preparation delivery process.

The NASDTEC outcome-based teacher education standards were developed at the transformational level of Spady and Marshall's hierarchy of outcomes (See Appendix - A).

This means that "curriculum content is no longer the grounding and defining element of outcomes (Spady & Marshall)." NASDTEC outcomes are *role performances* derived from *job analyses* of *beginning teachers* and expected of prospective teachers completing state approved teacher education programs. The impact of outcomes developed at the transformational level is that prospective teacher development is *verified in public school contexts and settings* prior to initial certification by the state certification/licensing authority.

Outcome-Based Standard Development

Standard

The Outcome Specification Model (WORKFORCE 2000, INC., 1991) was used to develop the format for the NASDTEC outcome-based teacher education standards. This model includes eight components for analyzing and describing an outcome statement. Its unique feature is the manner by which client needs, the teacher's expectations, and the purpose of the outcome are integrated into one statement. Appendix - B shows the model, its eight outcome specifications and their definitions, and one example of its use. The model has been adapted to include three distinct components for each standard: Client, Teacher Requirement, and Purpose.

This model is also based on the work that is being done related to "total quality," a client-driven approach to improvement. Applied in education, total quality means organizing and targeting all resources on activities that increase client satisfaction. In this context, quality is generally defined as meeting client needs and expectations. Moreover, total quality means ongoing improvement involving everyone, including but not limited to parents, students, teachers, principals, administrators, school board members, and teacher educators (Imai, 1986).

The primary message of total quality is that not a day should go by without some kind of improvement being made somewhere within a public school classroom and teacher education program. The NASDTEC outcome-based standards incorporate the client orientation of total quality as a way to integrate the total quality movement into national standards for teacher education and certification.

Authentic Context

Each outcome standard is followed by a paragraph that describes the context in which the outcome will be demonstrated and verified. The contexts are authentic because they represent the conditions of real teaching in elementary and middle level classrooms, schools, and communities. Taken together, the outcome areas for each level reflect the richness and the complexities of the beginning teacher's role in contemporary schools.

Sample Portfolio Entries

While Wolf (1991) describes a portfolio "as a container for storing and displaying evidence of a teacher's knowledge and skills, this definition is incomplete. A portfolio is more than a container--a portfolio also embodies an attitude that assessment is dynamic and that the richest portrayals of teacher (and student) performance are based on multiple sources of evidence collected over time in authentic settings" (p.130). Examples of teacher performance that might be used by states and institutions of higher education to verify the NASDTEC outcome-based standards are listed after each standard according to the following categories and definitions. The categories were selected and adapted to this portfolio approach from the Instructional Framework multi-media system for augmenting teacher behaviors (McTighe & Reeves, 1991).

During the development of the standards, NASDTEC members discussed whether the portfolio approach would be limiting and whether other sources of data might be used. They concluded that a portfolio could contain as many or as few items as a state might wish. It needs, also, to be emphasized that the proposed portfolio entries are SAMPLES. States may wish to specify the examples that it will require for each of the categories that it chooses to use.

- **Research** - A compilation of research findings and best practices related to the outcome area;

- **Video** - A series of video illustrations of the outcome area;

- **Lessons** - Example lesson and management plans used by the teacher to guide activities in the outcome area;

- **Assessments** - Example assessment instruments, processes, and approaches to documenting some aspect of the outcome;

- **Resources** - People, processes, and products used to demonstrate the outcome.

NASDTEC Outcome-Based Program Approval Model

The NASDTEC Tradition

Historically, NASDTEC standards have been used by its member states as a guideline or resource. Individual states have applied that guideline and embellished it for the specific development of their own standards and program approval processes.

According to the NASDTEC Standards For State Approval of Teacher Education (1989, revised edition), "States that have adopted the NASDTEC Standards rely on them in evaluating their professional preparation programs. Other states may use NASDTEC Standards as a framework to develop their own standards."

It is in this spirit that the outcome-based standards in this document are presented for use by states as an option or guideline. Thus, these outcome-based standards are expected to be considered in the context of other program approval procedures in use by states.

Each state utilizing the NASDTEC outcome-based standards still maintains the right to:

- exercise its state's right to define program approval requirements beyond those established by NASDTEC;

- conduct on-site visits, in addition to the application of standards;

- establish testing requirements, such as state-owned instruments or the NTE, as an additional measure of program success;

- establish specific admissions standards for colleges with teacher education programs;

- require specific areas of study be included within teacher.education programs;

- maintain special education requirements for teaching students with disabilities;

- add any of the above or additional information to assessments called for within the outcome-based standards structure.

Each state will want to examine carefully the need for process requirements when outcome-based standards are utilized. The data base from the outcome standards may encourage a state to provide flexibility to each of its training institutions to deal with the issue of "how to train teachers." This flexibility will be even more enhanced if the demonstrated outcomes rather than the completion of specific courses are required for certification. Colleges and universities would then be encouraged to explore new options for enhancing the quality of teacher training program effectiveness. In such a structure it would be important that a credit count approach to certification were not possible, or one could assume that "taking courses" would be viewed as an easier alternative to "demonstrated competence."

While outcome-based standards will provide many options for states to consider, there is no requirement or expectation that all states will wish to move in this direction. States using existing program approval procedures that consider college and university resources and curriculum have excellent accountability models in place.

A state that does wish to move toward outcome-based standards may still maintain many of its existing practices and policies. Simply adopting outcome-based standards does not mean that states cannot continue to maintain existing rules and regulations related to program approval (e.g. admission requirements, grade point average requirements, 10 weeks of full-time student teaching, site visits, etc.)

Recognizing that individual states may wish to phase in the implementation of outcome-based standards and program approval procedures, NASDTEC offers the following advice for those states seeking to fully implement the outcome-based standards. In the previous structure since specific areas of study and faculty qualifications were required, it was necessary to conduct on-site visits to ensure that the program met the standards. In an outcome-based design such reviews could become optional at a state's discretion since it is understood that the program must produce outcomes in order to have its graduates certificated.

At the heart of the implementation of an outcome-based program approval process must be assessment. The characteristics of such an assessment program should be authentic performance and portfolio. Such an approach would require the demonstrated ability to apply pedagogical knowledge and skills in real classroom settings.

Figure - 1 shows how authentic performance assessments differ from traditional assessments.

Such K-12 student assessments are currently being developed in Kentucky, Connecticut, Vermont, California, and Maryland. Within the area of teacher education the history of field experiences and student teaching have served as types of authentic assessment, which are now enriched by the addition of specified, measurable outcomes consistent with initial entry professional practice. Furthermore, state reform efforts have aligned outcomes of public schools and outcomes for teacher preparation.

Use of Portfolios

The most comprehensive assessment device for an outcome-based program approval structure is a portfolio strategy. The use of such a measurement strategy would allow the gathering of multiple measures throughout one's teacher preparation program. Such evidence would provide verification of skills as well as verification of ability to make applications with various types of students and in various settings.

The portfolio assessment strategy for prospective teachers allows them to:

- engage in extended activities relating instruction and assessment and practicing the art of self-assessment;

- make choices in their work and observe the effects of their choices;

TRADITIONAL	PERFORMANCE
➤ One mode, paper/pencil	➤ Multiple modes (Exhibitions, performances, portfolios, essays, interviews, observations)
➤ Administered in short, structured period of time	➤ Range in degree, structure, length, and resources
➤ Taps limited cognitive skills	➤ Taps range of abilities
➤ Limited learning dimensions	➤ Multidimensional
➤ Taps discrete skills	➤ Taps integrated abilities
➤ Atomistic	➤ Holistic
➤ Isolated event	➤ Ongoing event
➤ Decontextualized	➤ Contextualized

Source: Kruglanski, 1989.

FIGURE - 1

CHARACTERISTICS OF TRADITIONAL AND PERFORMANCE ASSESSMENT

■ look back at all of their work, examine the products, the processes, and strategies used to create them in order to determine which work is most characteristic of them as new teachers.

This material can also serve as the basis for assessment conferences with both public school and college faculties.

In this context the portfolio should be viewed as a container. This container could not only hold materials which the individual prospective teacher felt were exemplary, but also other information required by the institution or the particular state board of education or commission. This additional aspect of the portfolio could include such things as certification test requirements, grade point average information, citizenship requirements, or fingerprint records.

Program Approval

Within the context of both traditional and alternative teacher education programs, the main vehicle for program approval would be demonstrated professional practice. It would also be possible for a state's content knowledge standards to be aligned with those of the learned societies. Time would no longer be the variable that was held constant. The attainment of outcomes as specified in outcome-based standards would become the focus of programs. Hence, alternative training programs could be held to the same outcome standards, and thereby create a true alternative delivery system rather than a different set of outcomes from those of higher education institutions. The basic premises of portfolios for teacher education programs allow a training institution to:

■ provide evidence that each student is able to meet the standards prior to recommendation for certification. In this respect the portfolio serves the same purpose as a transcript which documents program completion components;

■ create benchmarks throughout the program to validate its effectiveness. Hence, it allows an institution to develop a total quality management approach to its programs with identified milestones that keep an individual student from proceeding through to the end of the program without benefit of diagnostic information.

The concept of portfolio in the NASDTEC program approval process flows from the work on portfolios funded through the Carnegie Foundation in the Stanford University Teacher Assessment Project (Wolf, 1991).

The final product of this portfolio structure would be a framework wherein each graduate has captured on videotape or videodisk high performance examples of each of the outcome areas in accordance with the data requirements established within the standards. That product may then be used with prospective employers and for initial staff development programs related to both beginning teacher and high quality licensure programs.

States that wish to use the outcome-based standards for the certification of individual candidates rather than for the approval of programs may use the portfolios to provide evidence that a person has demonstrated the outcomes needed to be certificated.

Each institution or alternative training structure seeking program approval would develop a portfolio system that responds to the following questions derived from the Carnegie Foundation-funded Teacher Assessment Project:

1. Given the NASDTEC outcomes, what is important for prospective teachers to document through the portfolio?

2. What form will the portfolio take?

3. What are the designated benchmarks during the program when progress will be measured?

4. What kinds of evidence will go into the portfolio?

5. How will the evidence be portrayed?

6. How should the portfolio entries be structured?

7. How much evidence is necessary and who decides acceptability of the portfolio contents?

8. How will the portfolio represent both growth and best work?

9. What other performances will be expected besides the portfolio?

10. What is the structure by which portfolios will be evaluated?

11. What will be the criteria for acceptability of portfolio entries?

12. How many unacceptable portfolios will cause a program to be disapproved?

Linking the total quality perspective to program approval would allow training program personnel to work collaboratively with classroom teachers and school district personnel to answer the 12 questions above and to more fully implement the outcome-based standards. This shared decision-making structure will be crucial to the development of programs that provide authentic contexts for demonstration of the standards through portfolio samples.

The importance of the portfolio as an assessment tool for program approval cannot be overemphasized. The Carnegie research demonstrated that "Portfolios enable teachers to document their teaching in an authentic setting and to bring in the context of their own classrooms in a way that no other form of assessment can" (Wolf, p. 136). Portfolios focus not only on the summative evaluative component, but also on the formative function. Not only are they indispensable in evaluating a teacher's pedagogical competence, but also hold the promise of reshaping the profession of teaching by holding teacher education programs accountable for demonstrated proficiency levels, including standards of performance as a condition of individual initial state certification.

Determining criteria for the acceptability of the portfolio entries should most appropriately be based on professional judgment. In recent years the emphasis in teacher education has been on correlational studies (where certain behaviors of teachers relate positively with certain behaviors of children). Recently, the shift has been to correspondence data (a normative view of teaching based on professional judgment rather than discrete studies). This movement has emerged in part because of the work of Lee Shulman and his colleagues in the Stanford Assessment Project where the complexity of teaching became the focus of their efforts.

This view of teaching accepts and honors the decisions of wise professionals. Under such a system, teachers identified by their peers as outstanding could work with colleges or universities and/or with state certification offices to establish minimum criteria for the portfolio entries.

The NASDTEC outcome-based standards should provide a direct connection between the expectations established by states for beginning teachers and the professional licensing assessments now being developed by the National Board for Professional Teaching Standards.

The NASDTEC Paradigm

The NASDTEC approach to standards is best understood in the context of a continuum where the traditional concept of teacher training is viewed as a series of courses where time and licensure are held constant and outcomes are variables. In the new framework, the outcomes are held constant and time and licensure are the variable entities.

Each of the outcome areas was selected by the NASDTEC Standards and Middle Level Committees because of its significance and is defined at the level and specificity of standards with which a national organization should be concerned (Figure - 2). This judgment was later confirmed by a review with high quality public school classroom teachers and principals from a school district noted for its outcome-based approach as a result of

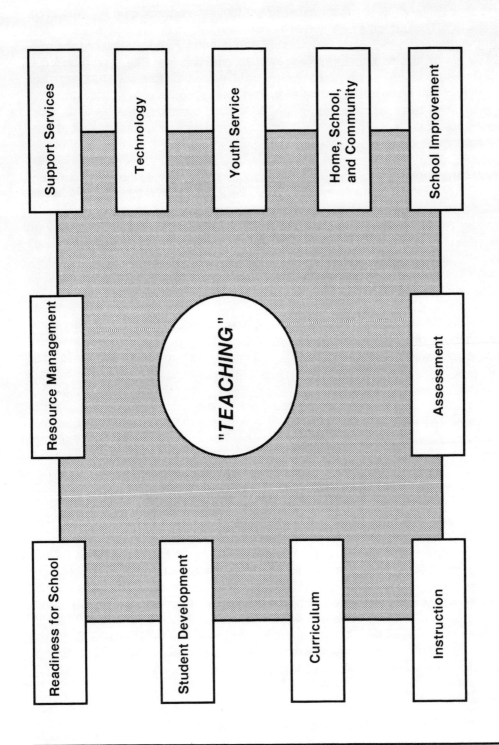

FIGURE 2

THE TEACHING ROLE AND RELATED OUTCOME STANDARD AREAS

some 3-5 years of work and training with Grant Wiggins of the University of Rochester, Lawrence Lezotte and his work with effective schools variables, and participation in a Carnegie funded proposal, including interagency cooperation in creating effective middle schools.

The specific outcome areas include:

- **Readiness for School** was identified directly from the *America 2000* goals and the priority being given to it by the Carnegie Foundation of New York as well as the significant body of data regarding the positive impact of early interventions on performance in school. The success of Headstart and its continued increase in funding by the federal government provides further impetus for moving in this area.

- **Student Development** was identified because of the importance of education being more than academic performance in schools. Virtually every part of the reform effort calls for developmentally appropriate education and a strong citizenry.

- **Curriculum** was identified as crucial because of the need for teachers and school-based educators to recognize that schools are organizations and that each teacher must be a member of a team working for the good of the program and common learning goals. The standard does not identify all areas of curriculum, but assumes alignment with national goals. Additional curriculum areas beyond those in the national goals should be identified by state departments of education, local school districts, and/or individual schools for the purpose of identifying programs to be delivered to students.

- **Instruction** was selected since it is at the heart of the education system. The standard does not identify all areas of instruction, but assumes alignment with national goals. Additional instructional areas beyond those in the national goals should be identified by state departments of education for teacher preparation and certification purposes.

- **Assessment** was recognized as a means of providing systematic feedback on the success of the total education program for purposes of adjustment, meeting standards, and continuous improvement.

- **School Improvement** was viewed as a means to achieve total quality in education. To achieve this mission, schools must work with professional educators, parents, the local community, and businesses. Schools must have the support of local communities, and to gain that support communities must feel the schools are theirs.

- **Support Services** was deemed essential insofar as it is crucial to coordinate the services of government and community agencies serving children, youth, and families. This is particularly important for the "at risk" student whose socioeconomic status and/or lack of parental concern or home support system causes continuous interference with the learning process.

- **Youth Service** was determined to be crucial in the context of helping students understand that the quality of one's life is related to developing strong social relationships and the necessity for individuals to work together harmoniously within a society.

- **Home, School, and Community** was determined to be a crucial factor for establishing the important early relationships between and among these three groups. The support system for public education requires that the home and community work together to reach common goals. All learning does not occur in the school, and therefore there must be a support structure beyond the school.

- **Technology** was added as a result of discussions with teachers and school-based administrators who felt that technology must not only be considered as a tool, but as a teacher, and that schools are not utilizing the full potential of technology for learning.

- **Resource Management** was included because beginning teachers are confronted with an array of responsibilities involving people, activities, and resources. School-based educators suggested that beginning teachers become skilled in project management techniques in order to be successful in this area.

A major feature of this model is that it can easily be adapted to the unique needs of any state. Additional areas can be added and/or eliminated as a state wishes. Also the Curriculum and Instruction areas can be subdivided to include specific curriculum areas that may be identified, (e.g. a state may wish to emphasize mathematics and reading at the elementary level or civics and career education at the middle level). These or any other subject related areas can be specifically included and addressed under the proposed Curriculum and Instruction areas.

SECTION - 2

ELEMENTARY LEVEL
OUTCOME-BASED STANDARDS

The Beginning Elementary Level Teacher

Social, economic, and demographic trends indicate significant changes in the nature and number of preschoolers in America. For example, each year more mothers enter the workforce, family values and structures change, the number of single-parent households increases, more children are affected by poverty conditions, and minority groups increase to the degree that they have become majority groups in some parts of the country. These changes are impacting the classroom setting of today's and future beginning elementary level teachers.

All children can learn. This fundamental premise challenges all teachers, especially today's beginning elementary level teacher. Depending on state policies governing entry to school and services to children with special needs, teachers may work with infants, toddlers, preschoolers, and/or young children up to age nine. In any case, teachers face a very complex set of individual student learning needs, interests, styles, developmental characteristics, and special challenges.

Elementary education is the beginning of the process of formal schooling. It provides the foundation for the intellectual, psychomotor, and social/emotional development of children. Teaching at this level should enable children to learn how to learn, assimilate and apply knowledge and skills, and interact positively with their peers and their environment. Learning should be interdisciplinary and provide both subject-based and subject-integrated experiences. Opportunities to develop positive self-concepts are necessary for continued success in school and life.

Teaching at the elementary level must be done in developmentally appropriate ways in which the teacher is a facilitator of learning. This includes but is not limited to, a balance of teacher-initiated and child-initiated activities, multisensory approaches, a variety of learning technologies, and independent and small group projects. The learning environment should encourage experimentation, risk taking, and acquisition of essential learning skills.

In this educational context, the teacher establishes a learning environment that welcomes children to school, facilitates their transition from a variety of backgrounds and experiences, and prepares each child for success in the middle learning years. The outcome-based standards contained in this section were designed to assist states in preparing beginning elementary level teachers for this type of learning environment.

STANDARD 1.0 - READINESS FOR SCHOOL

Client

For children to make a successful transition from family, child care, and/or preschool settings to a formal local school system,

Teacher Requirement

the beginning elementary level teacher during planning, delivery, and analysis activities translates and aligns classroom expectations, climate, and instructional practices with children's stages of readiness and developmental characteristics

Purpose

because children who start school ready to learn and receive developmentally appropriate instruction have the best chance for success.

AUTHENTIC CONTEXT

Rationale

A prevailing, fundamental premise of school reform is that every child can be successful in school. However, on one hand many children enter school affected by health risks such as low birth weight; prenatal exposure to alcohol, drugs, or smoking; lead poisoning; malnutrition; or child abuse and neglect. On the other hand, many children enter school with a rich background of parental support and with learning experiences involving a vast array of thinking skills. Both of these instances also occur when students transfer from one school to another. Other factors such as, but not limited to, the stability of the home, amount of love and affection, language acquisition, prior experiences in child care options, and self-concept add to the complex nature of each child that a beginning elementary level teacher will face and help to become a successful learner.

SAMPLE PORTFOLIO ENTRIES

- **Research** - A plan for determining and accommodating the readiness levels of each child assigned to the teacher;

- **Video** - Samples of nurturing a child's stages of adjustment over a prescribed period of time;

Outcome Documentation

- **Lessons** - Classroom activities for accommodating the different entry stages of academic, physical, and social development;

- **Assessments** - Identification of students who are having trouble socializing with other children because of transitioning into formal schooling or transferring into a new school;

- **Resources** - A directory of the people, print and non-print materials, and processes used to facilitate readiness.

STANDARD 2.0 - STUDENT DEVELOPMENT

Client

For children to build a strong foundation for learning,

Teacher Requirement

the beginning elementary level teacher during planning, delivery, and analysis considers, accommodates, and integrates the physical, social, emotional, cognitive, and linguistic developmental characteristics of elementary students

Purpose

to achieve positive self concepts; to master basic cognitive, psychomotor, and social skills; and to nurture the natural desire for learning.

AUTHENTIC CONTEXT

Rationale

Young children learn best in settings that are structured for the ways they develop and grow. The beginning elementary teacher must use knowledge about child development to identify and apply a wide range of developmentally appropriate behaviors, activities, and materials to accommodate each child's growth pattern, interests, talents, and experiences. This approach will lead to a learning environment that builds on initial entry to school and is responsive to the child's ongoing developmental patterns and potential to grow.

SAMPLE PORTFOLIO ENTRIES

■ **Research** - A journal containing a reflective analysis of the development of children under the teacher's supervision for an extended period of time;

■ **Video** - Samples of multiple learning settings, active learning, children working in computer stations, and small and large groups;

Outcome Documentation

■ **Lessons** - Small blocks of time are available for learning, activities are sensitive to multicultural differences, students have access to and use a variety of learning materials, learning styles are accommodated;

■ **Assessments** - Instruments for determining whether or not the learning climate is relaxed and open, learning goals are clear, and children are encouraged and challenged to learn;

■ **Resources** - Up to date materials such as bulletin boards are related to student interests, are posted at students' heights, and display student products.

	STANDARD 3.0 - CURRICULUM
Client	For the local school district requirement that its curriculum be interpreted and delivered to meet the needs of children,
Teacher Requirement	the beginning elementary level teacher in the certificated teaching assignment **analyzes and organizes into daily, weekly, monthly, and yearly teaching units developmentally appropriate, culturally sensitive, basic and higher order, challenging, and integrated subject matter including, but not limited to, reading and language arts, mathematics, science, humanities, history, geography, and healthy lifestyles**
Purpose	to ensure that what the employing school district expects to be taught and learned is delivered to meet the needs and interests of elementary level students.

AUTHENTIC CONTEXT

Rationale

Curricular trends in the elementary years will cause the beginning elementary teacher to structure curricular units to reflect subject-based, subject integrated, culturally sensitive, and thematic lessons in developmentally appropriate formats. National groups and state and local school systems prescribe the broad curricular frameworks that a teacher must interpret and deliver to students in the elementary years. The beginning elementary level teacher must translate the school's existing curriculum into "teachable" units and continuously improve them through feedback and additional knowledge.

SAMPLE PORTFOLIO ENTRIES

- **Research** - An analysis of local school system curricular models and trends that provide the rationale for a local school system's curriculum;

- **Video** - An explanation by the teacher about the approach taken to translate the local curriculum into teaching units for several subjects;

Outcome Documentation

- **Lessons** - Samples of short and long range lesson plans in integrated language development, reading, mathematics, and science for consideration by a potential employer;

- **Assessments** - Data summaries of lessons taught that are used to revise classroom curricular plans;

- **Resources** - A directory of people, print and non-print materials, and processes for students with special needs that were used to support the teacher's curricular units.

STANDARD 4.0 - INSTRUCTION

Client

For children to participate in instructional activities that accommodate their readiness for school and facilitate and result in learning,

Teacher Requirement

*the beginning elementary level teacher **elicits through effective teaching strategies, materials, and/or equipment the learning levels expected of students by the local school district in developmentally appropriate, culturally sensitive, basic and higher order, challenging, and integrated subject matter including, but not limited to, reading and language arts, mathematics, science, humanities, history, geography, and healthy lifestyles***

Purpose

so that students will have a positive self concept, a strong foundation in basic and higher order skills and subject matter, and preparation for successful transition to the middle years.

AUTHENTIC CONTEXT

Rationale

Teaching for learning in elementary classrooms should provide children with active, stimulating, interesting, and hands-on experiences. These experiences should relate to real world contexts that involve teamwork, integration, and problem-solving. Developmentally appropriate practices should guide the teacher in using direct, holistic, computer-based, cooperative learning, culturally sensitive, and real-life instructional approaches. Because of variables affecting children prior to entering school, the beginning elementary level teacher will need to adjust the levels of teaching to a variety of learning needs, styles, and paces. A major priority will be placed on helping all children achieve mathematics and science learning outcomes.

SAMPLE PORTFOLIO ENTRIES

■ **Research** - A review of the literature concerning effective teaching strategies for the elementary level that provides a rationale for the behaviors selected to teach a lesson(s);

■ **Video** - Segments of successful teaching lessons for discrete and integrated subjects, especially on mathematics and science topics, and segments which show sensitivity to different cultures;

Outcome Documentation

■ **Lessons** - A daily journal for monitoring and adjusting instructional strategies, classroom climate, and approaches for students with special needs and for reporting the results of instruction;

■ **Assessments** - Cooperating teacher feedback and self-assessments of classroom observational data that show teaching was adjusted to demonstrate that the teacher knows when students are ready to move on or need additional instruction;

■ **Resources** - Samples of student work resulting from the lessons that reflect practices that will be continued, modified, or extended in the future.

	STANDARD 5.0 - ASSESSMENT
Client	For children, their parents, and school district officials to determine readiness for school and the results of teaching for learning,
Teacher Requirement	the beginning elementary level teacher during planning, delivery, and analysis activities **develops assessments and interprets, applies, and reports the results of pre-kindergarten experiences and levels of functioning and classroom, district, state, and national assessments that measure readiness for school and the implementation of the school curriculum and its standards of performance for the teaching assignment**
Purpose	to yield information that increases the teacher's understanding of each child's readiness to learn; establishes high expectations, equitable monitoring, and explicit information about progress toward meeting standards; and targets interventions to move to higher levels of performance.

AUTHENTIC CONTEXT

Rationale

Assessment at the elementary level is multifaceted because of the influence and interaction of school readiness variables with the early learning and development of children. Hence, the beginning elementary level teacher should have a plan for comprehensive and descriptive assessments of student learning. The teacher's assessments should be sensitive to age, developmental stage, gender, language, culture, race, and socioeconomic differences among children. Assessment will consist of direct observation of student behavior, performance tasks, and teacher developed classroom techniques for relating student performance to parents, children, school and district officials, and the public.

SAMPLE PORTFOLIO ENTRIES

■ **Research** - Based on a review of effective assessments, a plan and timeline are developed for written, direct observation, and student performance-based classroom assessments for formative and summative purposes;

■ **Video** - Segments showing how teaching strategies were adjusted during classroom instruction to reflect data received from children, parents, principals, and school district officials;

Outcome Documentation

■ **Lessons** - Classroom assessment procedures and instruments are aligned with curriculum and instruction and accommodate students with special needs;

■ **Assessments** - The results of local and/or state assessments administered by the teacher are analyzed and reported in a user-friendly format and samples of classroom measures to assess student readiness and progress and the teacher's instruction are included;

■ **Resources** - People, print and non-print materials, and processes used to support teacher - designed, developed, field tested, and administered classroom criterion-referenced performance tasks.

Client

For an elementary school improvement structure comprised of teachers, the principal, parents, and community representatives to have meaningful and significant teacher participation in the school improvement process,

Teacher Requirement

*the beginning elementary level teacher as a collaborating participant **identifies, interprets, generates, and measures student readiness for school, group and individual developmental data, school improvement solutions, and progress***

Purpose

toward the continuous improvement of the school's culture, climate, and mission.

AUTHENTIC CONTEXT

Rationale

School improvement at the elementary level is a continuous process that empowers each school to both define and realize a vision of success for itself, all of its students, and the community. An elementary school's improvement plan should be based on shared values and visions. Achieving agreement on what a school does and why it does it, establishes a benchmark upon which to continuously improve. Throughout the United States individual schools are developing unique school improvement models designed to address their own specific improvement goals and a variety of local, state, and national school reform efforts. The beginning elementary level teacher must be ready to join these initiatives, participate substantively, and apply processes that implement the school's plan in classrooms.

SAMPLE PORTFOLIO ENTRIES

■ **Research** - A case study of one school's needs, goals, and processes for determining and implementing an action plan for improvement that involves relationships with preschool child care centers;

■ **Video** - A presentation of ideas concerning school improvement that were learned in a teacher preparation program and shared with a local school;

Outcome Documentation

■ **Lessons** - Plans for assisting and training the community to understand school improvement, especially through a school-based team approach;

■ **Assessments** - School improvement data disaggregated into understandable units and displayed for decision-making;

■ **Resources** - A newsletter produced for the community to learn about the activities of the school's improvement team.

Client

For families to assist their children to improve school performance,

Teacher
Requirement

the beginning elementary level teacher through home-school-community partnerships plans and contributes in providing social and emotional support to parents, exchanging information with them, improving and encouraging parent-child dialogue, and nurturing family involvement in children's education at home and in school

Purpose

because family support for education results in higher achievement and self esteem.

AUTHENTIC CONTEXT

Rationale

The profile of the American family has changed dramatically in the last decade. Over half of the American workforce in the future will be comprised of women with children under six. Nearly half the current workforce is made up of two-career couples and single parents. Moreover, approximately 25% of our children live in poverty. The need to build relationships between and among preschool settings such as child care centers, Head Start, and elementary schools with evolving home structures must be addressed to reverse the cycle of poverty, to establish foundations, and to provide on-going support for all students to reach higher educational expectations. The beginning elementary level teacher must be ready to contribute in activities such as creating positive home settings for learning, improving communications about grading, participating as a volunteer, counseling children about schooling, and contributing in school improvement efforts.

SAMPLE PORTFOLIO ENTRIES

■ **Research** - A survey of students and families is conducted and analyzed for determining the need for home-school-community partnerships;

■ **Video** - A plan is discussed by the teacher with a small group of parents for increasing communication about student performance;

Outcome
Documentation

■ **Lessons** - Multicultural issues/needs are reflected in classroom activities sensitive to differences in children, needs, and families;

■ **Assessments** - A strategy and instruments are developed to profile community demographics and to find out what the home settings of individual students are like in order to meet their special needs;

■ **Resources** - Appropriate use of a directory of child care centers and community agencies, organizations, and businesses that have committed to working with the school.

STANDARD 8.0 - TECHNOLOGY

Client

For children to participate in individualized learning and introductions to technology,

Teacher Requirement

the beginning elementary level teacher during planning, delivery, and analysis activities **correlates, integrates, and applies computer-supported learning and management systems in classroom teaching**

Purpose

to initiate or increase student knowledge about technology, to deliver direct instruction to all students at different levels and paces, and to use technology as a motivation for student learning.

AUTHENTIC CONTEXT

Rationale

At the elementary level students use technology to play, explore, create, and learn basic and higher order skills. Computers are used to teach children directly and as a supplement to the beginning elementary level teacher. Moreover, computers are useful for cross-age sharing between and among students and parents, as a learning station in the classroom, and as a means of facilitating family literacy programs. Teachers also use current and advanced technology to deliver and manage instruction and to perform administrative support functions. Because children are exposed to increasing uses of technology in homes, offices, supermarkets, malls, and other familiar places, they and their teachers need to be technologically literate.

SAMPLE PORTFOLIO ENTRIES

■ **Research** - An analysis of computer-supported approaches to teaching early learners is used to develop a plan for integrating the technology-based learning systems available in a school into settings for active learning;

■ **Video** - Segments are provided that show the teacher managing a cross-age computer activity with early learners;

Outcome Documentation

■ **Lessons** - Educational software applications for direct instruction are correlated with lesson plans and the developmental needs of students;

■ **Assessments** - The results of learning profiles generated by educational software are used to prescribe additional instruction;

■ **Resources** - A directory of people, software and hardware products and services, and vendors used to develop children's logical/mathematical thinking and language development.

STANDARD 9.0 - SUPPORT SERVICES

Client

For children and their families to access discrete or integrated support services from health, social, juvenile, human resources, and other community agencies,

Teacher Requirement

*the beginning elementary teacher during planning, delivery, and analysis activities **recognizes needs and refers students and their families to available in-school and community support service agencies***

Purpose

to ensure that all students are successful in educational programs.

AUTHENTIC CONTEXT

Rationale

The beginning elementary level teacher cannot produce learning on the part of students within the classroom alone. It is important that the teacher understand the support structure that is available both within and external to the school context. Comprehensive internal support services such as school nurses and counselors and external support services such as child support programs, medical screening, employment training, and family counseling help children and their parents achieve and maintain a stable environment. In this way the teacher works as part of a team and must clearly understand the roles of families and schools and the legal limits and responsibilities of the school.

SAMPLE PORTFOLIO ENTRIES

■ **Research** - An action plan for responding to the actual needs of a family and a list of the referrals made through the appropriate school channels;

■ **Video** - Samples of participation in an inter-agency team setting and a narrative by the teacher reflecting on the experience;

Outcome Documentation

■ **Lessons** - Sample lesson plans containing activities that address the needs of children who are waiting for special services;

■ **Assessments** - Signs of abuse including legal implications, behavior change, neglect, lack of academic growth, and attention deficits are identified and interpreted and a social service needs assessment is conducted for helping children and families;

■ **Resources** - A directory of legal, housing, crisis intervention, counseling, and health services in the community and summaries of referrals made to families.

AUTHENTIC CONTEXT

Rationale

The beginning elementary level teacher will be assigned many important classroom instructional and management duties and responsibilities. These will include in-school, community-based, and inter-agency projects and programs. Moreover, the teacher will act alone, as a team member, and in classroom settings involving children and parents. Because of this, it is imperative that the teacher be able to establish an objective, break assignments into phases, designate milestones, and report results. Also, the teacher will need to organize networks of people, tasks, and resources. Finally, the teacher should be able to calculate the costs of activities in order to build a realistic understanding of the return on investments of time, effort, and materials. This focus on the teacher as an effective manager of human, fiscal, and temporal resources is important given the public's expectation of a cost effective educational system.

SAMPLE PORTFOLIO ENTRIES

Outcome Documentation

- **Research** - A needs analysis and action plan for accomplishing role expectations across a specified period of time within schools and with community support groups;

- **Video** - A presentation of the teacher's project plan for opening and closing the school year;

- **Lessons** - Applications of time management contained in lesson plans;

- **Assessments** - An analysis of time spent on getting lessons started over an extended period of time and a plan for continuous improvement based on the findings;

- **Resources** - Printouts from project management software that were used to organize a unit of instruction.

SECTION - 3

MIDDLE LEVEL
OUTCOME-BASED STANDARDS

The Beginning Middle Level Teacher

Early adolescence today is significantly different from previous generations. Today's young adolescents live in a rapidly changing, technology-based world. They make decisions at a much earlier age about using tobacco, drugs, and alcohol; engaging in sexual activities; dropping out of school; and practicing healthy lifestyles. At the same time, they are struggling with rapid changes in their growth and development, with achieving a balance between dependence and independence, and with greater needs for peer acceptance.

According to the Carnegie Council on Adolescent Development and numerous state initiatives, middle level education should be delivered through small communities of learning. In these communities a core of common knowledge and interdisciplinary concepts are learned by all students because schools are committed to success for all students. Teachers and principals are empowered to restructure programs and the school. Schools promote good health practices and link them with the education and health of their students. Families work collaboratively with school staff. Schools and communities are partners in educating young adolescents. Teachers in these schools have been specifically prepared to teach young adolescents. Consequently, middle level education should lead students to a stronger commitment to school, positive social behavior, and productive personal development.

It takes a special kind of teacher to work with young adolescents. Whatever the instructional approach, the teacher must enjoy personal contact and involvement with young adolescents. Effective teaching at the middle level must be done in developmentally appropriate ways in which the teacher is a faciltator of learning, team member, and/or student advisor. This includes, but is not limited to, active teaching, cooperative learning, peer tutoring, project and group work, exploratory activities, basic and advanced learning technologies, and youth service.

In this educational context, the teacher establishes a learning environment that facilitates transition from the elementary learning years; fosters essential knowledge and thinking skills, creativity, exploration, communication, scientific literacy, and positive self-esteem; and prepares young adolescents for successful entry into high school and post high school learning opportunities. The outcome-based standards contained in this section were designed to assist states in preparing beginning middle level teachers for this type of learning environment.

STANDARD 1.0 - READINESS FOR SCHOOL

Client

For young adolescents to make a successful transition from the early learning years to the middle learning years,

Teacher Requirement

the beginning middle level teacher during planning, delivery, and analysis activities translates and aligns classroom expectations, climate, and instructional practices with young adolescents' stages of readiness and developmental characteristics

Purpose

because students are making a variety of transitions such as entering puberty, attending new schools, initiating new peer relationships, discovering self, establishing independence, and exploring new opportunities for learning.

AUTHENTIC CONTEXT

Rationale

A prevailing, fundamental premise of school reform is that every young adolescent can be successful in school. However, on one hand many children make the transition to the middle years without the essential skills, knowledge, and attitudes necessary to be successful. Moreover, some have been "held back," have developed negative attitudes toward schools and teachers, and have lost faith in school and family support. On the other hand, many children make the transition with a successful academic track record, positive self concepts, and enthusiastic family support. Both of these instances also occur when students transfer from one school to another at the middle level. Other factors such as, but not limited to, the stability of the home, amount of love and affection, status of peer group relationships, language development, and self-concept add to the complex nature of each young adolescent.

SAMPLE PORTFOLIO ENTRIES

- **Research** - A plan for determining and accommodating the readiness levels of each young adolescent assigned to the teacher;

- **Video** - Samples of working with a small group of young adolescents who are exploring options for career development and post high school study;

Outcome Documentation

- **Lessons** - Classroom activities for accommodating the different entry stages of young adolescents who are not performing according to a school's standards for middle level mathematics;

- **Assessments** - Identification of students who are having trouble learning in teams because of cultural differences;

- **Resources** - A teacher-developed handbook of effective practices to facilitate readiness throughout the middle learning years.

Client

For young adolescents to balance academic growth with social acceptance and self esteem,

*Teacher
Requirement*

*the beginning middle level teacher during planning, delivery, and analysis activities
considers, accommodates, and integrates the intellectual, physical, emotional,
psychological, and social developmental characteristics of middle level students*

Purpose

*to build upon and explore in a safe environment new knowledge, talents, positive attitudes
toward learning, social competency, and coping skills.*

AUTHENTIC CONTEXT

Rationale

Young adolescents change and grow dramatically during the middle years. They exhibit a variety of emotions and feelings often in the same day or class period. They are struggling to be successful during a very complex period of human development. They make decisions in areas such as academics, alcohol and drugs, sexual behavior, and school attendance that will affect their futures within and outside the school. Their interests, attention spans, and learning styles are diverse. The beginning middle level teacher must enjoy working with these students and be able to translate knowledge about their development into a wide range of developmentally appropriate behaviors, activities, and materials. This approach will lead to a learning environment that will facilitate each student's transition from childhood into adulthood.

SAMPLE PORTFOLIO ENTRIES

■ **Research -** Given a class of students, a personal development plan is designed that breaks out the students by need, provides an instructional unit, and explains why activities are organized as they are for particular students;

■ **Video -** Samples of teaching personal development lessons, including decision making and conflict resolution;

*Outcome
Documentation*

■ **Lessons -** A teacher advisor/advisee program is planned and conducted to facilitate regular student interaction with the teacher to share school-related topics in a non-instructional environment;

■ **Assessments -** Observations and data analyses by cooperating teachers of how student developmental characteristics are exhibited in teaching;

■ **Resources -** Focus groups are used to collect input from students about their needs and interests and are reflected in activities for the teacher to enhance interpersonal relationships with the students.

AUTHENTIC CONTEXT

Rationale

Curriculum in the middle years should help all young adolescents to develop positive self-concepts, think critically, develop healthful lifestyles, be active citizens in a culturally diverse society, integrate subject matter, and apply learning to real-world problems. National groups and state and local school systems prescribe the broad curricular frameworks that a teacher must interpret and deliver to students in the middle years. The beginning middle level teacher must translate the school's existing curriculum into "teachable" units and continuously improve them through feedback and additional knowledge.

SAMPLE PORTFOLIO ENTRIES

■ **Research** - An analysis of curricular models for nurturing self-concept at the middle level that provides the basis for a curricular unit designed by the teacher;

■ **Video** - A presentation that describes how a curricular plan, teaching activities, and assessments actually come together in an integrated lesson;

Outcome Documentation

■ **Lessons** - Samples of thematically-based interdisciplinary lessons plans;

■ **Assessments** - Curricular plans judged by several school department staff show that the student is a participating member of a curriculum team;

■ **Resources** - Example curricular plans that show the relationship between the school's essential core curriculum and every day life concepts.

AUTHENTIC CONTEXT

Rationale

Teaching for learning in middle level classrooms should provide young adolescents with active, exploratory, interesting, and hands-on experiences. These experiences should relate to real world contexts that involve teamwork, integration, and problem-solving. Developmentally appropriate practices should guide the teacher in using active teaching, cooperative learning, peer tutoring, thinking skills, teaming, computer-assisted, multiability groups, culturally sensitive, and real-life instructional approaches. Because of variables affecting the transition from the elementary level, the beginning middle level teacher will need to adjust the levels of teaching to a variety of learning needs, styles, and paces. A major priority should be placed on helping all students achieve higher levels of mathematics and science learning outcomes.

SAMPLE PORTFOLIO ENTRIES

■ **Research -** An analysis of videotapes of successful middle level teachers engaged in team teaching for consideration in augmenting teaching strategies;

■ **Video -** Samples of one-on-one and small group teaching strategies for helping young adolescents develop positive self concepts;

Outcome Documentation

■ **Lessons -** A management plan for delivering an interdisciplinary curricular unit with a team of teachers;

■ **Assessments -** Cooperating teacher feedback on the teacher's demonstration of active teaching strategies in mathematics and science;

■ **Resources -** A portfolio of appropriate exploratory program approaches including rationales used at the middle level for dissemination to other teachers.

AUTHENTIC CONTEXT

Rationale

Assessment at the middle level is multifaceted because of the need to determine the entry behaviors of children and to profile their progress through to the high school years. Hence, the beginning middle level teacher should have a plan for differentiated and descriptive assessments of student learning. The teacher's assessments should be sensitive to age, developmental stage, gender, language, culture, race, youth with special needs, and socioeconomic differences among children. Assessments will consist of direct observation of student behavior in classrooms and service sites, performance tasks, and teacher developed classroom techniques for relating student performance to parents, children, school and district officials, and the public.

SAMPLE PORTFOLIO ENTRIES

- **Research** - A review of multiple measures is completed to identify those that are appropriate for developing a profile of student learning;

- **Video** - Samples of student performance during youth service activities that document intended learning outcomes;

Outcome Documentation

- **Lessons** - Lesson plans demonstrate skill in aligning outcomes, objectives, activities, and assessments;

- **Assessments** - Samples of classroom measures used to assess student progress and instructional effectiveness and interpretations of international, national, state, and local results for organizing instruction;

- **Resources** - A handbook of measurement instruments, including performance assessments, developed by the teacher for real world contexts is produced.

STANDARD 6.0 - SCHOOL IMPROVEMENT

Client

For a middle school improvement structure comprised of teachers, the principal, parents, and community representatives to have meaningful and significant teacher participation in the school improvement process,

Teacher Requirement

*the beginning middle level teacher as a collaborating participant **identifies, interprets, generates, and measures group and individual student developmental data, school improvement solutions, and progress***

Purpose

toward the continuous improvement of the school's culture, climate, and mission.

AUTHENTIC CONTEXT

Rationale

School improvement at the middle level articulates with and builds upon the results of feeder elementary school teams. It is a continuous process that empowers each middle school to both define and realize a vision of success for itself, all of its students, and the community. This process contributes to the high school level. A middle school's improvement plan should be based on shared values and decisions linking the elementary and high school levels. Therefore, achieving agreement on what a school does and why it does it, establishes a benchmark upon which to continuously improve. Throughout the United States individual schools are developing unique school improvement models designed to address their own specific improvement goals and a variety of local, state, and national school reform efforts. Beginning middle level teachers must be ready to join these initiatives, participate substantively, and apply processes that implement the school's plan in their classrooms.

SAMPLE PORTFOLIO ENTRIES

- **Research** - School improvement needs are identified from multiple assessment data sources, including international, national, state, and local measures;

- **Video -** The teacher uses verbal and non-verbal behaviors supportive of team goals, needs, and requirements when interacting in the school improvement process;

Outcome Documentation

- **Lessons -** The knowledge base on effective schooling and teaching is reflected when generating solutions to school improvement needs;

- **Assessments -** Examples of teacher judgments, classroom tests and products, criterion-referenced assessments, and norm-referenced test results for school improvement purposes;

- **Resources -** A brochure produced for the community to learn about the elements of school improvement and the characteristics that make schools unique.

AUTHENTIC CONTEXT

Rationale

Generally, as children move into the middle years, parental involvement in their schooling declines. Consequently, middle schools must establish new approaches to reaching homes and communities. Teachers and families should work together and develop trust and respect for each other. Schools and communities, including the corporate/business sector, should coordinate resources for mutually beneficial purposes. Volunteer groups and individuals such as grandparents should be linked to school projects for addressing needs and goals. Parent-teacher conferences should focus on "customer needs" whereby the beginning middle level teacher relates professionalism, empathy, and knowledge in suggesting solutions. The teacher must also have proficiency in reporting to parents, and in making informal telephone calls regarding potential discipline or grade problems. In effect, the teacher must have skills in responding to the question from parents and community members, "What can I do?"

SAMPLE PORTFOLIO ENTRIES

Outcome Documentation

- ■ **Research** - A survey of homes, businesses, and community agencies to determine who will contribute volunteer services for a specific project;

- ■ **Video** - Samples of conferencing skills with parents and other volunteers in real and simulated environments;

- ■ **Lessons** - A plan for demonstrating proficiency in dealing with irate parents in a productive manner;

- ■ **Assessments** - Samples of ways to report information and grades to parents so as to solicit their support for the education program;

- ■ **Resources** - Input from other teachers identified and collected before contacting a student's parents thereby demonstrating the ability to work collaboratively in an interdisciplinary manner.

STANDARD 8.0 - TECHNOLOGY

Client

For young adolescents to participate in individualized learning and wider applications of technology,

Teacher Requirement

the beginning middle level teacher during planning, delivery, and analysis activities **correlates, integrates, and applies computer-supported learning and management systems in classroom teaching**

Purpose

to broaden student knowledge about technology, to deliver direct instruction to all students at different levels and paces, and to use technology as a motivation for exploration and higher order learning.

AUTHENTIC CONTEXT

Rationale

At the middle level, students use a variety of basic and advanced learning technologies to learn subject matter and higher order skills at their own paces. Moreover, students use computer software applications such as word processing, spreadsheets, data bases, and graphic interfaces to create solutions and solve problems in all subjects. The beginning middle level teacher becomes a mentor as students increase their use of technology as a support system for learning. As the students make the transition to the high school years, they have accepted technology as an integral part of their approach to learning. In the middle school, computers are a resource to the teacher for managing instruction and administrative tasks.

SAMPLE PORTFOLIO ENTRIES

■ **Research** - A plan for integrating the technology-based learning systems available in a school into settings for active learning;

■ **Video** - Segments are provided that show the teacher mentoring a student in the use of computer application packages;

Outcome Documentation

■ **Lessons** - Graphic interfaces are used to illustrate learning outcomes in mathematics and science;

■ **Assessments** - An analysis of several data base software packages is completed through a team approach involving students and teachers;

■ **Resources** - A directory of people, software and hardware products and services, and vendors used to operate a computer "users group."

AUTHENTIC CONTEXT

Rationale

The beginning middle level teacher cannot produce learning on the part of students within the classroom alone. It is important that the teacher understand the support structure that is available both within and external to the school context. Comprehensive internal support services such as in-school health clinics, counselors, and advisor/advisee relationships and external support services such as youth servicing agencies, drug and pregnancy prevention programs, work training, and recreation centers help young adolescents and their families achieve and maintain a stable environment. In this way the teacher works as part of a team and must clearly understand the interrelated roles of parents, school personnel, and support service providers. These roles must be implemented within the legal limits and responsibilities of the school.

SAMPLE PORTFOLIO ENTRIES

■ **Research** - A review of research studies focused on inter-agency coordination and an action plan for implementing recommendation for promising practices;

■ **Video** - Samples of discussions with representatives from youth serving agencies including a narrative by the teacher reflecting on the experience.

Outcome Documentation

■ **Lessons** - Sample lesson plans containing activities that show how support service agency resources are accessed and used by families and individuals;

■ **Assessments** - The results of an informal survey conducted on the effects of an inter-agency approach to providing services within the school;

■ **Resources** - A directory of support services judged by families and students to be the most effective for meeting their needs.

Client

For the local school system requirement that its teaching staff be responsible, efficient, and professional,

Teacher Requirement

*the beginning middle level teacher during planning, delivery, and analysis activities **plans, schedules, and manages roles, objectives, phases, and milestones of teaching assignments in the public schools***

Purpose

in order to have a successful preparation program.

AUTHENTIC CONTEXT

Rationale

The beginning middle level teacher will be assigned many important classroom instructional and management duties and responsibilities. These will include in-school, community-based, and inter-agency projects and programs. Moreover, the teacher will act alone, as a team member, and in classroom settings involving children and parents. Because of this, it is imperative that the teacher be able to establish an objective, break assignments into phases, designate milestones, and report results. Also, the teacher will need to organize networks of people, tasks, and resources. Finally, the teacher should be able to calculate the costs of activities in order to build a realistic understanding of the return on investments of time, effort, and materials. This focus on the teacher as an effective manager of human, fiscal, and temporal resources is important given the public's expectation of a cost effective educational system.

SAMPLE PORTFOLIO ENTRIES

Outcome Documentation

- ■ **Research** - A needs analysis and action plan for accomplishing role expectations across a specified period of time within middle schools and with community support groups;

- ■ **Video** - A presentation of the teacher's project plan for opening and closing the school year;

- ■ **Lessons** - Applications of time management contained in lesson plans;

- ■ **Assessments** - An analysis of time spent on getting lessons started over an extended period of time and a plan for continuous improvement based on the findings;

- ■ **Resources** - Printouts from project management software that were used to organize a unit of instruction.

Client

For young adolescents to feel needed and valued in making contributions,

Teacher Requirement

the beginning middle level teacher within the school or outside with local agencies, businesses, and community organizations **organizes, operates, and continuously improves a youth service prcgram**

Purpose

for the students to develop positive self-concepts and an awareness of and concern for others and to become productive, caring, and effective citizens.

AUTHENTIC CONTEXT

Rationale

An important function of the middle school is to "connect with the community." Within the school, communities of learning are structured to support student academic, social, and personal development. Youth service is one way for students to extend these communities and to become aware of the importance of others to their lives and to their own quality of life. The beginning middle level teacher must play a role in formulating these values by clearly making a linkage between instruction and the community. Additionally, college students in their preparation programs should be involved in community activities themselves in order to serve as a role model.

SAMPLE PORTFOLIO ENTRIES

- **Research** - A survey study of local agencies and organizations willing to participate with the school that serves as the basis of a plan for developing the concept of youth service with a group of young adolescents;

- **Video** - Samples of the teacher leading discussions of students who are reflecting on the activities and results of their youth service projects;

Outcome Documentation

- **Lessons** - A sequence of lessons for preparing students to initiate their youth service projects;

- **Assessments** - An analysis of the impact of the youth service programs conducted by the teacher's students including recommendations for improvement;

- **Resources** - A publication describing the purposes, operation, and impact of a variety of youth service programs at the national, state, and local levels.

SECTION - 4

NASDTEC LEADERSHIP AND ASSISTANCE

NASDTEC Leadership and Assistance:
Teacher Education Quality Improvement Framework

The Teacher Education Quality Improvement Framework shown in Figure - 3 provides a way for NASDTEC and its clients to work toward the common goal of implementing the outcome-based standards. Using this framework, or other similar planning tools, each state can develop a unique outcome-based system designed to address its own specific initiatives while it draws on the wisdom, "lessons learned," and assistance of NASDTEC and other states.

This Framework was adapted from the work of states and local districts implementing school improvement and professional development projects for school reform (State School Improvement Team, 1991). The essential elements of a state outcome-based teacher education system are grouped under three categories in the first column: *How To Examine* your state, *What To Examine* in your State, and *What Makes Your State Special?* The essential elements shown under the categories are illustrative examples only. Each state could adopt these, amend them, or add new elements to meet its particular needs and goals.

Key questions for completing the Framework are noted across the top of the columns. When the Framework is used to guide planning, a vision and structure for outcome-based teacher education come forth for achieving state goals and initiatives. In effect, the Framework helps a state to identify its current status and direction, needs, and desired end product for implementing outcome-based teacher education. Each state's product will be different. Through its leadership and assistance roles, NASDTEC could collect similar planning tools from the states and facilitate their use to meet client needs.

The continuous improvement of leadership and assistance should help NASDTEC and its clients to see the desired results of collaborative efforts with outcome-based teacher education and certification.

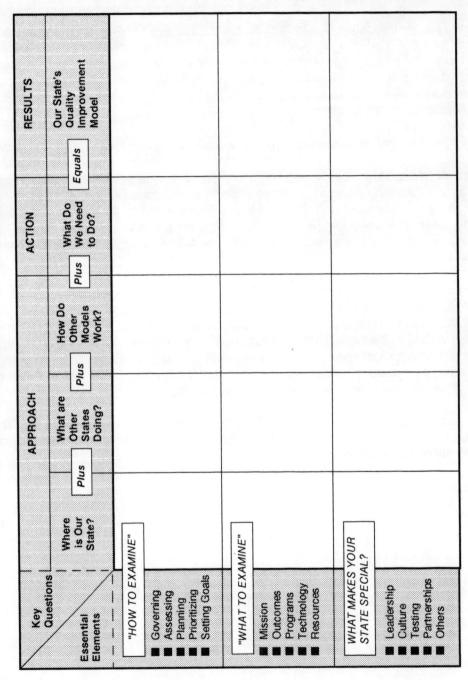

FIGURE - 3
TEACHER EDUCATION QUALITY IMPROVEMENT FRAMEWORK

SECTION - 5

REFERENCES

References

Abt Associates Inc. (1991). *Working with Families: Promising Programs to Help Parents Support Young Children"s Learning* (Contract No.: LC88088901). Washington, DC: U.S. Department of Education, Office of Planning, Budget, and Evaluation.

America 2000. An Education Strategy. (1991). Sourcebook. U.S. Government Printing Office.

Berliner, D. (undated). *The Development of Expertise in Pedagogy.* Arizona State University and Spencer Fellow Center for Advanced Study in the Behavioral Sciences.

Berry, T. H. (1991). *Managing the Total Quality Transformation.* New York: McGraw-Hill.

Boyer, E. L. (1991). *Ready to Learn: A Mandate for the Nation.* Princeton: The Carnegie Foundation for the Advancement of Teaching.

Bridgman, A. (1989). *Early Childhood Education and Child Care.* Arlington, Virginia: American Association of School Administrators.

Carlzon, J. (1987). *Moments of Truth: New Strategies for Today's Customer-Driven Economy.* New York: Harper & Row.

Carnegie Council on Adolescent Development. (1989). *Turning Points: Preparing American Youth for the 21st Century.* New York: Carnegie Corporation of New York.

Division of Instructional Learning Systems. (1980). *Programmatic Definition for Middle Childhood Education.* Charleston, West Virginia: West Virginia Department of Education.

Division of Professional Development Systems. (1980). *Designing County Continuing Education Training Programs for Middle Childhood Educators.* Charleston, West Virginia: West Virginia Department of Education.

Educational Standards, Testing, and Access. (1985). *Proceedings of the 1984 ETS Invitational Conference.* Educational Testing Service, Princeton, New Jersey.

Gagne, J. (1986). *America's Quality Coaches.* Dow-sponsored special report in the March edition of *CPI Purchasing* magazine.

Hohmann, C. (1990). *Young Children & Computers.* Ypsilanti, Michigan: The High Scope Press.

Imai, M. (1986). *Kaizen: The Key to Japan's Competitive Success.* New York: McGraw-Hill.

Irvin J. L. (Ed.). (1992). *Transforming Middle Level Education: Perspectives and Possibilities.* Boston: Allyn and Bacon.

Kruglanski, H. (1989). *Performance Assessment: What? and How?, The Common Core of Learning Assessment.* Presented at Windsor, Connecticut, for the CONNECTIONS states consortium.

Levitan, S. A., Mangum, G. L., & Pines, M. W. (1989). *A Proper Inheritance: Investing in the Self-sufficiency of Poor Families.* Washington, DC: The George Washington University, Center for Social Policy Studies.

Making the Middle Grades Work. (1988). A Publication of the Adolescent Pregnancy Prevention Clearinghouse. Children's Defense Fund.

Maryland Commission on the Early Learning Years. (1992). *Laying the Foundation for School Success: Recommendations for Improving Early Learning Programs in Maryland.* Baltimore: Maryland State Department of Education.

Maryland Task Force on the Middle Learning Years. (1989). *What Matters in the Middle Grades: Recommendations for Maryland Middle Grades Education.* Baltimore: Maryland State Department of Education.

Mastain, R. K. (Ed.). (1992). *Manual on Certification and Preparation of Educational Personnel in the United States.* National Association of State Directors of Teacher Education and Certification. Kendall/Hunt Publishing Company, Dubuque, Iowa.

McTighe, J. & Reeves, B. (1991). The Instructional Framework: A Computer-Based Resource for Informing Practice. *Journal of Staff Development*, Fall, Volume 12, No. 4, 38-41.

National Association of State Directors of Teacher Education. (1989, Revised Edition). *Standards for State Approval of Teacher Education.*

National Board For Professional Teaching Standards (1991). The Vision of the National Board. *Brochure*, April.

National Board For Professional Teaching Standards. (undated paper). *Toward High and Rigorous Standards for the Teaching Profession: Initial Policies and perspectives of the National Board for Professional Teaching Standards*. 3rd Edition.

National Task Force on School Readiness. (1991). *Caring Communities: Supporting Young Children and Families.* Alexandria, Virginia: National Association of State Boards of Education.

Office of Technology Assessment. (1988). *Power On! New Tools for Teaching and Learning.* Washington, DC: Congress of the United States, Office of Technology Assessment.

Pankratz, R. (1991). *Kentucky's New Vision for Schools: Valued Outcomes and Performance Assessment.* A paper presented at the NASDTEC Annual Conference in Bellevue, Washington.

Presidents' Commission on Teacher Education (November, 1991). American Association of State Colleges and Universities. *Teach America: A Presidents' Agenda for Improving Teacher Education.*

Schalock, D. (1991). *A Framework for Thinking About the Place of Student Learning in Evaluating the Competence of Beginning Teachers.* A paper presented at the NASDTEC Annual Conference in Bellevue, Washington.

Spady, W. & Marshall, K. (1991). *Seven Models of Outcome-Defined OBE Curriculum Design and Delivery.* The High Success Program on Outcome-Based Education. Eagle, Colorado.

State School Improvement Team. (1991). *Framework for the Future: Creating Better Schools.* Baltimore: Maryland State Department of Education.

The Commission on Teaching Standards for School Mathematics. (1991). *Professional Standards for Teaching Mathematics.* National Council of Teachers of Mathematics.

The National Middle School Association. (1989). *NCATE - Approved Curriculum Guidelines: Basic and Advanced Programs in Middle Level Teacher Education.* Columbus, Ohio: National Middle School Association.

Villegas, A. M. (1991). *The Praxis Series. Professional Assessments for Beginning Teachers. Foundations for Tomorrow's Teachers - No. 1: Culturally Responsive Teaching.* Princeton: Educational Testing Service.

Warger, C. (Ed.). (1988). *A resource Guide to Public School Early Childhood Programs.* Alexandria, Virginia: Association of Supervision and Curriculum Development.

Wolf, K. (1991). The Schoolteacher's Portfolio: Issues in Design, Implementation, and Evaluation. *Phi Delta Kappan*, October, 129-136.

WORKFORCE 2000, INC. (1991). *Outcome Specification Model.*© Cockeysville, Maryland: Permission to use in NASDTEC Outcome-Based Standards and Portfolio Assessment granted to NASDTEC by WORKFORCE 2000, INC.

SECTION - 6

APPENDICES

APPENDIX - A

CURRICULUM DESIGN	DRIVING CONCEPTS

CURRICULUM DESIGN AS LIFE EXPERIENCE

THROUGH Continuous
  Journaling/Enactment Logs
  Life Role/Context Diaries
  Imagineering
  Peoplewatching
  Dialogue/Interviews
  Reflection

Phenomenological Perspective

Designers As Strategic Learners, Investigators

Designer Self-Assessment as Learning

CURRICULUM AS INSTRUCTIONAL DESIGN

THROUGH
  Knowledge as Design Process

  Frameworking Concepts

  Restructured Information

  Process Models

Designers As Coordinators, Collaborators,
  Consultants

Assessment As Learning

Assessment As Credentialing

CURRICULUM AS COMPLIANCE

VIA
  Document Guides

  Reference Manual Mindset

  Instructional Objectives Lists

  Test Analysis

Articulation Accountability

Teachers As Document Producers

Student Evaluation For Credentialing

TRANSFORMATIONAL

7. Life-Role Performances Requiring Synthesis and Application of Higher-Order Processes and Concepts in Authentic Life Contexts are CulminatingOutcomes

6. Role Performances Apply Higher-Order Processes and Concepts Across Settings and are Used as Culminating Outcomes

TRANSITIONAL

5. Higher-Order Processes and Concepts are Integrated as Culminating Outcomes, Problems, Questions, Unifying Themes, etc.

4. Higher-Order Processes are Culminating Outcomes and Integrate Common Concepts and Competencies Across Content Categories

3. Existing Subject Categories Incorporate Higher-Order Processes "As Appropriate"

TRADITIONAL

2. Subject Categories Drive Outcomes as in Curriculum "Cycles"

■ Cumulative/ Comparative   ■ Low-Level Scores   ■ Grade Alignment

1. Content Specifics and Activities Drive Outcomes

■ "Testing"   ■ Low-Level   ■ Minimum Alignment

Source: Spady & Marshall, 1991

APPENDIX - B

OUTCOME SPECIFICATION MODEL©

OUTCOME SPECIFICATIONS WORKSHEET

==

- **OUTCOME AREA:**

- **CUSTOMER:**

- **CUSTOMER NEEDS/REQUIREMENTS:**

- **TEACHER:**

- **CONTEXT/CONDITIONS:**

- **TEACHER REQUIREMENTS:**

- **SUBSTANCE:**

- **PURPOSE:**

==

STANDARD

Developed by Workforce 2000, Inc. - 1991

OUTCOME SPECIFICATION MODEL©

DEFINITIONS OF OUTCOME SPECIFICATIONS

===

- **OUTCOME AREA:** A component of the beginning teacher's role that is identified through a job analysis.

- **CUSTOMER:** A person who buys a product or experiences a service with certain needs and requirements in mind.

- **CUSTOMER NEEDS/REQUIREMENTS:** The lack of anything requisite, desired, or useful.

- **TEACHER:** the person who produces and delivers products and services on time to meet customer needs and requirements.

- **CONTEXT/CONDITIONS:** The on-the-job professional setting in which the outcome standard must be demonstrated, assessed, and verified.

- **TEACHER REQUIREMENTS:** The specific role performance(s) expected of the teacher while engaged in the substance.

- **SUBSTANCE:** The tasks, content, procedures, and/or functions of the education profession provided through the outcome standard.

- **PURPOSE:** The intended result of performing the outcome standard.

===

Developed by Workforce 2000, Inc. - 1991

OUTCOME SPECIFICATION MODEL©:
APPLIED TO NASDTEC OUTCOME-BASED
ELEMENTARY LEVEL STANDARDS

OUTCOME SPECIFICATIONS

==

- **OUTCOME AREA:** Readiness for School

- **CLIENT:** For children

- **CLIENT NEEDS/REQUIREMENTS:** to make a successful transition from family, child care, and/or preschool settings to a formal local school system

- **TEACHER:** the beginning elementary level teacher

- **CONTEXT/CONDITIONS:** during planning, delivery, and analysis activities

- **TEACHER REQUIREMENTS:** translates and aligns

- **SUBSTANCE:** classroom expectations, climate, and instructional practices with children's stages of readiness and developmental characteristics

- **PURPOSE:** because children who start school ready to learn and receive developmentally appropriate instruction have the best chance for success.

==

READINESS FOR SCHOOL STANDARD

For children to make a successful transition from family, child care, and/or preschool settings to a formal local school system, the beginning elementary level teacher during planning, delivery, and analysis activities **translates and aligns classroom expectations, climate, and instructional practices with children's stages of readiness and developmental characteristics** *because children who start school ready to learn and receive developmentally appropriate instruction have the best chance for success.*

This example was developed by Workforce 2000, Inc. for NASDTEC